The Sweet Spot: In Pursuit of Steady-state Greatness

By Joseph Thomas Plummer

For America

"The greatness of America lies not in being more enlightened than any other nation, but rather in her ability to repair her faults."
– Alexis de Tocqueville

The Force.

"The universe looks more and more like a great thought rather than a great machine." – Sir James Jeans

In 1902, James Jeans put forth a theory in astrophysics that today seems applicable to economic theory. Jeans suggested that there is some radius of a cloud of interstellar dust where thermal energy per particle equals gravitational work per particle. At this critical length, the cloud does not expand or contract. Perhaps more significantly, Jeans suggested that if a cloud lacked the necessary thermal energy, or pressure, to counteract the gravitational force, then the cloud would begin a process of runaway contraction. While this analogy might not be clear at first glance, the idea of "runaway contraction" is something that can be easily understood in the context of economics. In economics, we fear runaway contraction like the plague. More precisely, we fear runaway contraction in economics, because we know what it leads to – The Great Depression.

By extension, "the gravitational force" in this analogy would be a summation or confluence of symptoms or conditions that effectively cause the degradation of quality of life. In other words, the gravitational force, or economic entropy, is the natural force of economic deterioration. Perhaps it can best be understood by the value of a car being driven off a dealership lot. Likewise, after a building is built, it will begin deteriorating. After a road is paved, it will begin deteriorating. After a shirt is sewn, it will begin deteriorating. All things have life cycles. Some are longer than others, but in general once something is created, it begins to deteriorate.

Suppose we were to create a new society on Mars. Also, suppose that the environment on Mars doesn't produce any usable materials. We can only use what we bring. We might bring enough materials to build 10 great buildings, pave 10 great roads, and sew everyone matching outfits. The moment we have built 10 great buildings, 10 great roads, and sewn everyone matching outfits will be the peak of quality of life on Mars, unless new usable materials are introduced. From the moment those things are created, they begin to degrade. And, that is the gravitational force.

The "thermal energy" or "pressure" counteracting the gravitational force of economic deterioration is the creative force applied by humans to survive and thrive. This is the force applied by humans to constantly improve quality of life. If the gravitational force is the deterioration of wealth and value, then the thermal energy or pressure necessary to prevent runaway contraction is the creation of wealth and value. Perhaps more precisely, it is human creativity and productivity that counteracts the gravitational force of economic deterioration. In the words of John Connor, "If you are listening to this, you are the resistance."

There are many questions that are raised from this line of thought. Will current societal trends lead us to a point where the gravitational force of economic deterioration is greater than the force of human creativity and productivity? If we reach that point, will there be a real risk of runaway contraction? Can we make societal changes that will insure the force of human creativity and productivity is always greater than the gravitational force of economic deterioration? What is our end game? It is the opinion of this author that societal trends are leading us to a point where the gravitational force of economic deterioration will be greater than the force of human creativity and productivity, and when we reach that point, there will be a very real risk of runaway contraction. Furthermore, it is the opinion of this author that we can make societal changes that will insure the force of human creativity and productivity is always significantly greater than the gravitational force of economic deterioration, and we should define our end game as steady-state greatness.

The role of money.

"The importance of money flows from it being a link between the present and the future." – John Maynard Keynes

Money is a good thing. It allows us to function as a society. Money allows us to do many things. It allows us to compare the value of any product or service to the value of a sandwich. The deli down the street charges five dollars for a sandwich, and the painter charges $200 to paint a room in my house. So, the value of a freshly painted room will be roughly the same as 40 sandwiches. Money also allows us to store value at a very low cost. If we had to barter, we might have to store crops or materials that could be traded, and that would mean we would need to store these materials, transport them, and market them. This would add considerable costs to every transaction. But, the ability to store value is good for more than just reducing transaction costs. The ability to store value allows us to think about the future. We can save value at a very low cost, and we can pivot very easily and very quickly. Instead of being constrained by the nature of our assets, we can easily develop interests, businesses, knowledge, and ultimately more value to individuals and society as a whole. Money is a good thing.

Money has some very unique characteristics (standardized, widely-accepted, easy to carry, etc.). Perhaps the most important characteristic of money is that it is divisible. We can give the deli a 20-dollar bill for our sandwich and they will give us back 15 dollars and a delicious sandwich. The divisibility of money allows us to be precise in our transactions. For individuals and businesses, this precision allows us to reach economic equilibriums in day-to-day commerce. The deli owner can optimize his profit. The customer can compare two different five-dollar sandwiches and decide which one is better. The divisibility of money allows value optimization and market competition to thrive. The divisibility of money also allows for efficient public finance. For example, if a small town needed to tax its citizens in order to maintain the town's infrastructure, then a sales tax could be implemented in a way that only marginally increased the price of sandwiches. The small sales tax, while negligible to the deli owner and the sandwich eater, would accumulate a substantial amount of money that the town could use to maintain its infrastructure.

Money is simply a representation of value. Everything in the universe has a value. Things can have positive value or negative value. For example, sandwiches have a positive value, and diseases have a negative value. We pay to have sandwiches, and we pay to not have diseases. If we wanted to, we could assign a dollar value to everything we know. So, if everything in the world has value, does that mean that the amount of money in the world is equal to the sum of all of the positive value plus the absolute value of the sum of all of the negative value? No. Friendship has a very high value, but it is often given to us for free. Volunteers provide value, but we don't pay for their services. The environment provides value, but most of the time we don't pay for it. So, how do we know how much money should exist in the world? This is the great question.

In order to answer this question, we need to understand the demand for money. Think about an individual's demand for money. Of course most individuals have an infinite demand for money. This is a combination of an individual's need and want for money. Consider basic human needs- food, water, shelter, clothing, medicine, etc. Now consider basic human desires- entertainment, learning, career development, security, interaction, etc. Let's say basic human needs and desires on average are $50,000 per person per year. Multiply that by 300 million people. The result is 15 trillion dollars. Would that be a sufficient money supply? We can assume that the value of materials to make products and services is included in the 50k. But, how does each person get the 50k? Where does the money originate? And, where does it go? The flow of money over time must be considered.

Let's pretend when we land on Mars there is no money. Let's say in time period zero, T_0, no money exists. Then in time period 1, T_1, the government creates all of the money supply it thinks necessary and splits it evenly among its citizens. Then as time progresses people spend some of their money and earn some of it back. The smart and lucky ones accumulate significant amounts of money far above the original 50k. And, the dumb and unlucky ones aren't able to replenish their money from year to year and eventually aren't able to pay for basic human needs. What happens next?

The government and society as a whole have some basic decisions to make. The first decision is deciding if this income disparity, and the poverty associated with it, is acceptable. Are we ok with a significant number of people not being able to pay for basic human needs? The next decision is what to do about it. The government has some options. 1) Do nothing. 2) Implement taxes and government programs that effectively alleviate poverty. 3) Increase the money supply. Society has similar options. 1) Do nothing. 2) Give time and creativity to solve the disparity. 3) Give money to the poverty alleviation programs. Option 1 in both sets is unacceptable. Some combination of the remaining options must be considered.

Every person has a propensity to spend, a propensity to save, and a propensity to give money (and other things like time and creativity). When individuals save money, the effective money supply decreases. In other words, when people accumulate money far above the average, and then don't spend it, the economy is essentially operating with less money. Granted, banks may be investing the money that is be saved by individuals, but those investments generally do not influence poverty alleviation, infrastructure maintenance, or environmental restoration (though they could). This doesn't mean saving is bad for society. In fact, saving is a good thing. Saving allows us to do bigger and better things. This would mean that as the rate of saving increases, if we want to keep the effective money supply constant, then we would have to inject more money into the economy. But again, even if we keep effective money supply constant, that doesn't mean that every person will have his or her needs met. If the government increases money supply without changing anything else, poverty will remain virtually unscathed over time.

There are other variables that should be manipulated to decrease poverty. There is some optimal level of money supply that exists where poverty is eliminated by the right kind of capitalism, reasonable taxes, an optimal societal propensity to give, and effective poverty alleviation methods. At this level of money supply, it does not make sense to increase the amount of money in the system, because every person's basic needs are met. And, it does not make sense to decrease the money supply, because this would cause some individuals to fall below the poverty line. All individuals live above the poverty line. The rich are still far richer than most others, but every person has their basic human needs met. So, how do we determine this optimal level of money supply? And, is poverty the only problem we are trying to solve by optimizing money supply? We need a more thorough understanding of money demand.

A fixed pie.

"Most economic fallacies derive from the tendency to assume that there is a fixed pie, that one party can gain only at the expense of another." – Milton Friedman

Demand often corresponds to willingness to pay. There are sandwiches at the deli for five dollars, and there are 100 sandwich eaters that are willing to pay five dollars or more for one of those sandwiches. If the price were raised to six dollars, there might only be 75 sandwich eaters willing to pay. In the case of money demand, the concept of willingness to pay does not translate well. Money is the medium of exchange, and not the object for which we are exchanging. On a typical supply and demand graph, if an object is produced at a level lower than the optimal, then there is a deadweight loss that can be quantified. The money market graph that is typically referred to is not useful in this conversation. This model does not give us the information we need.

We want to find out where money demand becomes static and the rate of change is close to zero. This is where no increase in money supply will increase or decrease the demand for money. To find this point we can construct a simple graph that has money supply and money demand on the y-axis and time on the x-axis. This construct will yield a curve that helps us understand the relationship between money supply and money demand. This is a nice graph, but we still don't know how to find money demand. The current definitions and constructs related to money demand are obsolete. These definitions and constructs were developed before the information age, before the highway interstate system, before we landed on the moon, and before climate change.

For a healthy economy to exist, interest rates, the velocity of money, price levels, and income must all be given attention. However, in developing a definition for the demand for money, none of those variables are directly relevant. We need to think about demand for money in a different way. How much money would exist in an ideal society?

The demand for money is likely some function of at least the following variables: 1) society's propensity to give, 2) society's propensity to save and make long term investments, 3) society's propensity to spend and make short term investments, 4) federal debt, 5) the amount and condition of public infrastructure, 6) the environment, 7) population, 8) human health, 9) poverty, and 10) resiliency. This is probably not an exhaustive list, but this will get us started. This is a lot of variables to manage. These variables are defined and discussed below.

MD = Money Demand
MS = Money Supply
S_G = society's propensity to give
S_A = society's propensity to save
S_P = society's propensity to spend
$S_G + S_A + S_P = 1$
MS_E = effective money supply = $(1 - S_A) \times MS$
D = federal debt in dollars
I_Q = amount of infrastructure in dollars
I_C = condition of infrastructure
I_D = infrastructure demand for money = $I_Q \times (1 - I_C)$
P_0 = population
P_Q = amount of dollars required to meet basic human needs and wants
P_D = population demand for money = $P_0 \times P_Q$
H_H = human health (disease)
H_N = poverty
H_D = humanitarian demand for money = $H_H + H_N$

E_Q = environmental quantity in dollars
E_C = environmental condition
E_D = environmental demand for money = $E_Q \times (1 - E_C)$
R = resiliency

The propensity to give, save, and spend are self-explanatory, but it is important to note that the sum of the three variables is equal to one. Society's propensity to save determines the effective money supply. Society's propensity to give influences, but does not determine, the amount of poverty. This is because we cannot say definitively that a dollar given to a poverty alleviation program reduces poverty by one dollar or at all.

The federal debt will be used as an indicator and variable of demand. This is based on the premise that federal debt should not exist. If the federal government goes into debt it is for some combination of the following reasons:

1. Insufficient revenue model (taxes, fees, etc. have not been optimized)
2. Unforeseen expenses (wars, natural disasters, the plague, etc.)
3. The scope of the federal government grows (new legislation passes that requires the government to do more than it has in the past)

In any case, it is conceivable to construct a resilient system where debt is not necessary because of long term planning and designated reserves allocated for specific purposes, such as, rehabilitating roads and bridges (public infrastructure), defeating Nazis, or rebuilding cities destroyed by hurricanes.

The size and scope of public infrastructure is continuously changing, but we know that insufficient funding can result in catastrophic failures. This necessitates inclusion in our money demand model. The infrastructure demand for money, I_D, is equal to the value of all public infrastructure in dollars multiplied by one minus the condition of that infrastructure. The condition of infrastructure is quantified by a number between 0 and 1, where the infrastructure is in perfect condition at 1.

Population effects money demand. Imagine if we had kept money supply constant over the past 200 years while population grew exponentially. Another way to think about this is considering a ratio of money supply to population, similar to a ratio of GDP to population. So, if population increases by one, then the money supply should increase to keep the ratio constant. If we don't increase money supply when population increases, then we are effectively causing deflation.

The humanitarian demand for money, H_D, is perhaps the most difficult variable to quantify. What we are trying to capture is the amount of money necessary to eliminate diseases and poverty. The trouble with attempting to quantify these is that every person that has a disease and every person that lives in poverty is different. For example, it might take one thousand dollars to cure one person of a disease, but two thousand dollars to cure a different person of that same disease. In the context of poverty, it might take thousands of dollars to get one person out of poverty, while a different person might just need a simple opportunity. Humanitarianism often times lacks perfect information, which results in inefficiencies. However, changes in infrastructure, environment, and giving can decrease the humanitarian demand for money. For now, quantifying humanitarian demand for money is a shot in the dark.

Environmental demand for money is also difficult to quantify, but it is feasible to quantify the value of the environment. We know generally the value of the services that the environment provides. So, when we degrade the environment, we can determine the lost value. The problem with this method of quantification is that in reality the cost of fixing the system can be higher than the lost value, especially in the short run. For now, we will quantify environmental demand for money by multiplying some environmental value in dollars, E_Q, by one minus the condition of the environment, E_C. This will give us a rough idea of how much money we need to restore the environment to its prime.

The final variable is resiliency, R. This variable is also based on the premise that federal debt should not exist. If federal debt does exist, then it would function as the resiliency variable up to the given debt ceiling. There is no way to know the exact amount of resiliency demand for money. If an asteroid hits the earth, then we are probably going to need a little bit more than if a category 5 hurricane hits the Gulf Coast. However, we can try to predict the number of hurricanes and the amount of damage they will cause from year to year. We can try to predict how many wars and conflicts per century we will be engaged in. We can try to predict how many times the stock market will crash per century. Accounting for resiliency in our money demand model allows us to develop a more sustainable monetary system that reflects preparedness.

Our final equation for money demand is the sum of all of the variables. In the most ideal world, money demand is equal to population demand for money. The remaining demand variables are taken care of (reduced to zero) by the right kind of capitalism, reasonable taxes, and society's propensity to give.

$$MD_r = D + I_D + P_D + H_D + E_D + R$$

Equilibrium is reached when money demand equals effective money supply. It is important to note that money demand does not need to equal effective money supply tomorrow. But, money demand and effective money supply need to be closer to equal tomorrow than they were today. That would be considered progress.

The tool and the driver.

"Money is only a tool. It will take you wherever you wish, but it will not replace you as the driver." – Ayn Rand

We now have a money demand model that makes sense. What should we do with it? We know debt is over 16 trillion dollars. Infrastructure and environmental demand for money are both increasing. Humanitarian demand for money is not zero. And, resiliency has simply not been considered. Should we create some amount of money in excess of 16 trillion dollars and inject it into the system tomorrow? No. That is a recipe for hyperinflation.

Our current construct for creating money, quantitative easement, is ineffective and does not address infrastructure, environmental, and humanitarian demand for money in a timely manner. Our process of creating and injecting money into the economy needs to change. The following three methods could be used in combination to effectively address all of the variables in our money demand model in a timely manner, 1) the resiliency method, 2) the capacity building method, and 3) the straight-line method. The resiliency method addresses resiliency, R. The capacity building method addresses humanitarian demand, H_D. And, the straight-line method addresses infrastructure and environmental demand, I_D and E_D. It is also worth mentioning that investments in technology, research and development, and/or education have the potential to reduce demand for money on all fronts.

The resiliency method suggests that money should be injected in to the system immediately following disasters for the purposes of rebuilding. If a town is completely destroyed by a tornado, then money is injected for the specific purpose of rebuilding the town. The amount of money injected is dependent on society's propensity to give and the amount of government resources available to support the rebuilding process. After Hurricane Katrina, volunteers went down to the Gulf Coast for years to rebuild homes and infrastructure. Likewise, the government supported rebuilding efforts in various ways. However, as disasters happen more frequently, we will test the limits of society's propensity to give and government resources, which will necessitate the resiliency method.

The capacity building method focuses on the potential of the nonprofit sector to address the humanitarian demand. Within the nonprofit sector, there are organizations that provide goods and services for free, and there are also organizations that have robust revenue models that pay for the goods and services. In both cases, the nonprofit sector effectively addresses humanitarian demand. If we want to reduce humanitarian demand to zero, then we either have to make poverty alleviation (and the like) profitable, or we need to expand the capacity of the nonprofit sector and increase society's propensity to give. The capacity building method suggests that we create money and inject it directly into the nonprofit sector for the sole purpose of expanding long-term capacity. None of this money can be used for programs, because that would not change long-term outcomes. The money has to be exclusively for capacity building. This could look very differently from organization to organization. One organization might develop a new revenue model, while another might make a large capital investment. Expanding the capacity of the nonprofit sector will also reduce the need for government programs. It is conceivable that the nonprofit sector could take on all non-governing functions of the government.

The straight-line method addresses infrastructure and environmental demand. Again, a combination of the right kind of capitalism, reasonable taxes, and society's propensity to give should be sufficient to maintain infrastructure and the environment. However, when we degrade the environment and allow infrastructure to break, we are creating significant demand. If we don't maintain properly, then the infrastructure and the environmental demand for money will increase. The straight-line method suggests that we create money for prioritized infrastructure and environmental rehabilitation projects. These are projects that are well-beyond typical maintenance and thus require a different funding stream so as to not break the back of the government budget. The straight-line method also addresses the potential of inflation by spreading the money injection over an extended period of time. This extended period of time also allows for lower priority projects to be addressed in innovative ways before high-level intervention.

It is important to note that in all three methods, creating more money than necessary has the potential to have a negative impact on the economy by causing unnecessary inflation. Also, unless humanitarian, environmental, infrastructure, and resiliency demand for money are all zero, it will always makes sense for society to increase its propensity to give. Therefore, we should also consider methods of increasing society's propensity to give. Consider these five methods of increasing propensity to give, 1) philanthropy education, 2) shared value, 3) incentives, 4) recognition, and 5) marketing. Philanthropy education is just like any other education. If you want more scientists, teach more science in public schools. If you want more philanthropists, teach more philanthropy in school. Increasing propensity to give through shared value is very effective as individuals that give also get value. Benefit concerts are a great example of shared value where individuals buy tickets and enjoy the concert, but instead of the ticket revenue benefiting the bands and the venue, the concert benefits a cause. Incentives, like tax breaks, encourage giving by reducing the financial impact to the individual. Recognition is self-explanatory. Marketing is an effective way to increase giving, as most people are not aware of all of the humanitarian needs that exist. With marketing and philanthropy education there are significant costs that should be considered.

The real measure.

"The real measure of your wealth is how much you'd be worth if you lost all your money." –Anonymous

If society is to continue to progress, it will be the result of long-term planning and wide spread understanding of the system of systems that make up our world. Money has been the focus of this discussion, but money is not the measure of our society's greatness. Money is like water for the tree of society. If you pour too much on, you will drown the tree. If you don't pour enough on, you will starve the tree. You have to give the tree the right amount of water, and you have to make sure the water reaches the roots of the tree. We don't know what the fruits of optimizing the money supply will be. But, we know that if we find that sweet spot, then we can begin our pursuit of steady-state greatness.

Playing with numbers.

"No amount of experimentation can ever prove me right; a single experiment can prove me wrong." – *Albert Einstein*

The following scenarios have been constructed to explore the dynamics of money supply and some of the variables related to money demand. The first three scenarios explore ratios of money supply to population and money supply to infrastructure quantity. These scenarios do not take into account the condition of the population or the infrastructure.

Scenario 1

Time	People	Roads	Money	Environment	Money to People	Money to Roads
0	0	0	0	1	N/A	N/A
1	2	1	100	1	50.0	100.0
2	4	1	100	1	25.0	100.0
3	4	2	100	1	25.0	50.0
4	10	4	100	1	10.0	25.0
5	100	10	200	1	2.0	20.0
6	500	20	200	1	0.4	10.0
7	1000	50	500	1	0.5	10.0
8	900	50	500	1	0.6	10.0
9	900	60	750	1	0.8	12.5
10	1000	65	1000	1	1.0	15.4

Scenario 2

Time	People	Roads	Money	Environment	Money to People	Money to Roads
0	0	0	0	1	N/A	N/A
1	2	1	100	1	50.0	100.0
2	4	1	100	1	25.0	100.0
3	4	2	200	1	50.0	100.0
4	10	4	400	1	40.0	100.0
5	100	10	1000	1	10.0	100.0
6	500	20	2000	1	4.0	100.0
7	1000	50	5000	1	5.0	100.0
8	900	50	5000	1	5.6	100.0
9	900	60	6000	1	6.7	100.0
10	1000	65	6500	1	6.5	100.0

Scenario 3

Time	People	Roads	Money	Environment	Money to People	Money to Roads
0	0	0	0	1	N/A	N/A
1	2	1	100	1	50.0	100.0
2	4	1	200	1	50.0	200.0
3	4	2	200	1	50.0	100.0
4	10	4	500	1	50.0	125.0
5	100	10	5000	1	50.0	500.0
6	500	20	25000	1	50.0	1250.0
7	1000	50	50000	1	50.0	1000.0
8	900	50	45000	1	50.0	900.0
9	900	60	45000	1	50.0	750.0
10	1000	65	50000	1	50.0	769.2

The following two scenarios consider humanitarian demand in the form of disease. In these scenarios, society's propensity to give is not considered. Scenario 4 shows a base case where money supply is not tied to population growth. Scenario 5 considers money supply growth directly related to population growth, but not diseased population. Both scenarios tabulate ratio of money to diseased population. These scenarios were developed to begin to consider the implications of disease and human health on money demand.

Scenario 4

Time	People	Diseased Population	Money	Environment	Money to Diseased People
0	0	0%	0	1	N/A
1	2	0%	100	1	N/A
2	4	25%	100	1	100.0
3	4	50%	100	1	50.0
4	10	40%	100	1	25.0
5	100	10%	200	1	20.0
6	500	15%	200	1	2.7
7	1000	20%	500	1	2.5
8	900	10%	500	1	5.6
9	900	50%	750	1	1.7
10	1000	1%	1000	1	100.0

Scenario 5

Time	People	Diseased Population	Money	Environment	Money to Diseased People
0	0	0%	0	1	N/A
1	2	0%	100	1	N/A
2	4	25%	200	1	200.0
3	4	50%	200	1	100.0
4	10	40%	500	1	125.0
5	100	10%	5000	1	500.0
6	500	15%	25000	1	333.3
7	1000	20%	50000	1	250.0
8	900	10%	45000	1	500.0
9	900	50%	45000	1	100.0
10	1000	1%	50000	1	5000.0

In just the first five scenarios developed, we can begin to understand how money supply might have a significant impact on quality of life and how human population, health, infrastructure, and the quality of the environment might effect the demand for money. Likewise, the need for long-term planning is very apparent. There are also some curious questions that arise. For example, can we decrease money demand by making investments in technology and research and development? Is it possible to reduce money demand to zero without increasing money supply? People are naturally more creative and efficient when they are constrained, so how long should we wait before increasing the money supply?

These scenarios also don't consider how money exists in the system. In all scenarios, society's propensity to give would reduce money demand. In addition, there are scenarios where money demand exists that could be solved by optimizing a revenue model. For example, it is possible that there is infrastructure demand for money, because the government has not developed a sufficient revenue model for infrastructure. And, revenue models can become more and less effective overtime. For example, the commonly referred to gas tax or carbon tax will undoubtedly be effective in the short run, but insufficient in the long run. This is because as we become more and more fuel efficient and maybe one day independent of fossil fuels our revenue will decrease to a point where it doesn't pay for what we want it to, which may be road maintenance or environmental restoration. This will happen with any Pigouvian tax. The more effective the tax in changing behavior, the more unreliable the revenue will be in the long run. The purpose of a Pigouvian tax isn't to be a robust revenue model though. In the case of environmental demand for money, it is possible that a situation could exist where if a negative action stopped occurring, then the environment would heal itself, but it could also go the other way. Unlike infrastructure, where the damage is generally permanent, the environment, at least in some cases, has the ability to fix itself thus lowering the money demand to restore it.

To answer to the purpose.

"The great secret of succeeding in conversation is to admire little, to hear much; always to distrust our own reason, and sometimes that of our friends; never to pretend to wit, but to make that of others appear as much as possibly we can; to hearken to what is said and to answer to the purpose." – Benjamin Franklin

What's next? Have we solved the riddle? Was it already solved before we got here? There is a logical end to this line of thought, but this document is not that end. Rather, this document is the first inquiry of a young economist in search of that end. It is quite possible that this line of thought has already been exhausted, and the solution set has already been discovered. If this is the case, then perhaps monetary theory is not relevant in the context of poverty alleviation, infrastructure, and the environment. If this is not the case, then perhaps increasing the amount and visibility of conversation related to monetary theory and economic idealism will yield a more ideal society.